UNCOVERING TH[E]
ANALYZING PRIMARY SOUR[CES]

McCARTHYISM AND THE RED SCARE

HEATHER C. HUDAK

 Crabtree Publishing Company
www.crabtreebooks.com

Author: Heather C. Hudak

Editor-in-Chief: Lionel Bender

Editors: Simon Adams, Ellen Rodger

Proofreaders: Laura Booth,
Wendy Scavuzzo

Project coordinator: Petrice Custance

Design and photo research: Ben White

Production: Kim Richardson

**Production coordinator and
prepress technician:** Ken Wright

Print coordinator: Margaret Amy Salter

Consultant: Amie Wright,
The New York Public Library

**Produced for Crabtree Publishing
Company by Bender Richardson White**

Photographs and reproductions:
AP Images: front cover, Wikimedia: front cover bkgd (NYT), Alamy: 22 (Everett Collection Historical), 25 Top (Everett Collection Historical): Getty Images: 1 (Library of Congress), 4–5, 5 (H. Armstrong Roberts), 6–7 (Martha Holmes), 8–9 (Toronto Star Archives), 13 (Universal History Archive), 14 (Amanda Edwards), 15 Top (John D. Kisch/Separate Cinema Archive), 15 Btm (Gene Lester), 16-17 (Getty Images), 20–21 (Bettmann), 23 Left (AFP), 23 Rt (Library of Congress), 24 (MPI), 25 Btm (AFP), 28–29 (The LIFE Picture Collection), 30–31 (Gary Leonard), 34 (Bettmann), 41 (Pool): Library of Congress: 3 (LC-DIG-ppmsca-24370), 16, 18 Top Left (Icon) (LC-DIG-ds-07186); National Archives:10–11 (President's Secretary's Files, Truman Administration), 32–33 (Records of the United States Senate; Record Group 46); PA Images:38–39 (ABACA/PA Images), 40–41 (SIPA USA/PA Images); Shutterstock: 4, 6 Top Left (Icon) (Tutti Frutti), 8, 10, 12, 14 Top Left (Icon) (Bisual Photo), 20, 22, 24, 26, 28, 30 Top Left (Icon) (spatuletail), 32, 34, 36 Top Left (Icon) (David Reilly), 38, 40 Top Left (Icon) (Rena Schild); Topfoto: 7 (AP/Topham), 12, 19, 26, 27, 29, 37 (The Granger Collection), 30 (The Image Works), 35 (Topham Picturepoint), 36 (AP/Topfoto); Wisconsin Historical Society Library US Government Publications: 18. **Map:** Stefan Chabluk

Cover photo: Joseph McCarthy gestures during a Senate subcommittee hearing on McCarthy's charges of communist infiltration of the U.S. State Department. **Cover background:** A clipping of the *New York Times* story of the Overman Committee report. **Title page photo:** Joseph McCarthy

Library and Archives Canada Cataloguing in Publication

Hudak, Heather C., 1975-, author
    McCarthyism and the Red Scare / Heather Hudak.

(Uncovering the past : analyzing primary sources)
Includes bibliographical references and index.
Issued in print and electronic formats.
ISBN 978-0-7787-3939-5 (hardcover).--
ISBN 978-0-7787-3943-2 (softcover).--
ISBN 978-1-4271-1998-8 (HTML)

    1. McCarthy, Joseph, 1908-1957--Juvenile literature. 2. Anti-communist movements--United States--History--20th century--Juvenile literature. 3. Internal security--United States--History--20th century--Juvenile literature. 4. Subversive activities--United States--History--20th century--Juvenile literature. 5. United States--Politics and government--1945-1953--Juvenile literature. 6. United States--Politics and government--1953-1961--Juvenile literature. I. Title.

E743.5.H78 2017   j973.9   C2017-903629-7
                                         C2017-903630-0

Library of Congress Cataloging-in-Publication Data

Names: Hudak, Heather C., 1975- author.
Title: McCarthyism and the red scare / Heather Hudak.
Description: New York, New York : Crabtree Publishing Company, [2018] |
Series: Uncovering the past : analyzing primary sources |
    Includes bibliographical references and index.
Identifiers: LCCN 2017024399 (print) | LCCN 2017024985 (ebook) |
    ISBN 9781427119988 (Electronic HTML) |
    ISBN 9780778739395 (reinforced library binding) |
    ISBN 9780778739432 (pbk.)
Subjects: LCSH: Anti-communist movements--United States--History--20th century--Juvenile literature. | McCarthy, Joseph, 1908-1957--Juvenile literature. | Internal security--United States--History--20th century--Juvenile literature. | Subversive activities--United States--History--20th century--Juvenile literature.
Classification: LCC E743.5 (ebook) | LCC E743.5 .H77 2018 (print) | DDC 973.9--dc23
LC record available at https://lccn.loc.gov/2017024399

Crabtree Publishing Company

www.crabtreebooks.com   1-800-387-7650

Printed in Canada/082017/EF20170629

Published in Canada
Crabtree Publishing
616 Welland Ave.
St. Catharines, ON
L2M 5V6

Published in the United States
Crabtree Publishing
PMB 59051
350 Fifth Avenue, 59th Floor
New York, NY 10118

Published in the United Kingdom
Crabtree Publishing
Maritime House
Basin Road North, Hove
BN41 1WR

Published in Australia
Crabtree Publishing
3 Charles Street
Coburg North
VIC, 3058

UNCOVERING THE PAST

THE PAST COMES ALIVE

"No one man can terrorize a whole nation unless we are all his accomplices."

TV journalist Edward R. Murrow on the CBS show
See It Now on March 7, 1954.

In the late 1940s and 1950s, many Americans feared the Soviet Union wanted to take over the world and spread its **communist** ideals. In a communist **society**, there is no private ownership. The state, or government owns and controls almost all business and property. That was very different from the democratic and **capitalist** society of the United States which emphasized personal freedom and private owership of property and business.

During this time of heightened fear, Joseph McCarthy, a Republican senator from Wisconsin, spent five years investigating the U.S. government in search of anyone who had communist sympathies and loyalties. He accused hundreds of people of communist **subversion** and disloyalty. This led to a widespread belief that Soviet **spies** had **infiltrated** the U.S. government and society. McCarthy's determination to seek out subversives brought him into prominence and power. This period of time is known as the Second Red Scare. The extreme approach McCarthy used to interrogate people became known as McCarthyism.

The Red Scare and McCarthyism influenced people and politics in a way that continues to shape society today. To understand these events, we study history. History is everything that happened in the past, including only yesterday. Historians look for information, clues, and **evidence** from events. They **analyze** and interpret this material to help explain the cause and effects of things. Information about the past is found in many sources, including libraries, **archives**, newspapers, museums, and private collections.

▶ The **economy** of the United States and Canada boomed after **World War II** (1939–1945). Many people were able to buy houses and cars. But the threat of war with the U.S.S.R. hung overhead like a nuclear cloud. There was a real fear that communism would spread and change our way of life.

DEFINITIONS

Union of Soviet Socialist Republics (U.S.S.R.): A communist country in Northern Asia and Eastern Europe that was made up of Russia and 14 other countries.

Soviet: A term used to describe anything related to the U.S.S.R.

Communism: An economic and political system in which all property is owned by its members and is used for the good of all people.

Capitalism: An economic and political system in which trade and industry are privately owned.

▲ At the height of the **Cold War** of the 1950s and 1960s, many Americans feared a physical war with the Soviets that would result in the use of nuclear weapons, such as this atomic bomb explosion.

THE FIRST AND SECOND RED SCARES

Communists were typically associated with Russia and the U.S.S.R. and called "Red" because of the color of the Soviet flag. The term *Red Scare* has been used to describe a fear of communism or extreme **leftist** political beliefs. It refers to two periods in history when people in the United States and Canada became concerned about the potential rise of communism in their countries. In a communist society, all wealth and resources are owned by the government and shared among the people. Individuals cannot own property, farms, or factories. The goal of communism is to create a society without **class** divisions.

The First Red Scare took place in the early 1900s. In 1917, during **World War I**, the Russian Empire's economy was crumbling. The czar, or ruler, was forced to give up his throne. The Duma, or government, was replaced temporarily. However, many people in Russia were still unhappy. Food was scarce, prices were high, and working conditions poor. People wanted Russia to leave the war. A **revolution** led to the government being overthrown. It was replaced by a communist system under the **Bolshevik** political party. The new government took Russia out of the war and changed people's lives. Some Americans were inspired by the revolution and believed a **socialist** government in the United States could solve problems such as poverty.

Years later, the Second Red Scare was brought on by the start of the Cold War. The U.S.S.R. was an ally of the United States and Canada during World War II. After the war, the U.S.S.R. and the United States became the world's super powers. They had different **ideologies**

▲ In October 1947, ten well-known U.S. writers and movie directors were accused of communist activities. They were sentenced to jail time and banned from working at the major Hollywood studios. These Hollywood actors flew in to Washington, D.C., in support for the "Hollywood Ten."

"There are today many Communists in America. They are everywhere—in factories, offices, butcher stores, on street corners, in private businesses. And each carries in himself the germ of death for society."

J. Howard McGrath, President Truman's attorney general, in 1949

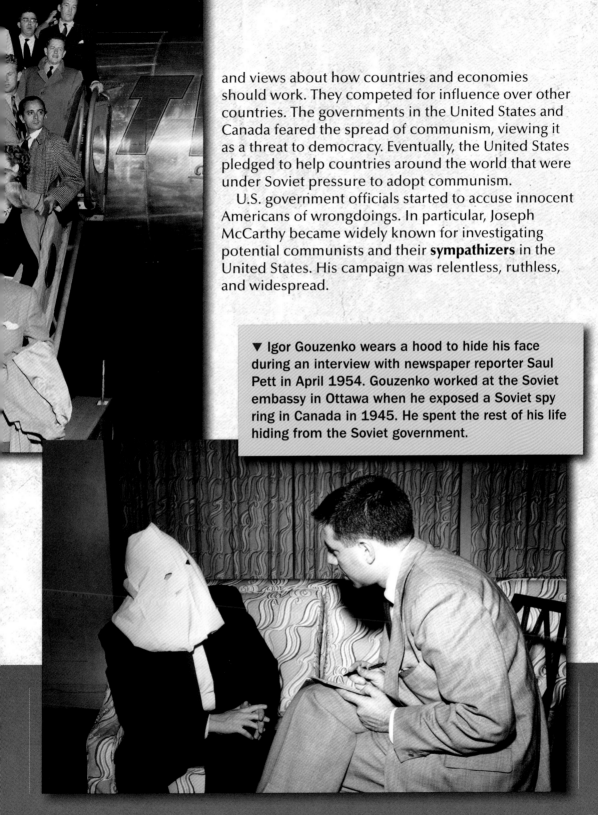

and views about how countries and economies should work. They competed for influence over other countries. The governments in the United States and Canada feared the spread of communism, viewing it as a threat to democracy. Eventually, the United States pledged to help countries around the world that were under Soviet pressure to adopt communism.

U.S. government officials started to accuse innocent Americans of wrongdoings. In particular, Joseph McCarthy became widely known for investigating potential communists and their **sympathizers** in the United States. His campaign was relentless, ruthless, and widespread.

▼ Igor Gouzenko wears a hood to hide his face during an interview with newspaper reporter Saul Pett in April 1954. Gouzenko worked at the Soviet embassy in Ottawa when he exposed a Soviet spy ring in Canada in 1945. He spent the rest of his life hiding from the Soviet government.

TYPES OF EVIDENCE

"Facts are stubborn things; and whatever may be our wishes, our inclinations, or the dictates of our passion, they cannot alter the state of facts and evidence."

John Adams, politician and future U.S. president, in 1770

Historians require evidence of past events to be able to understand them. Evidence is a collection of facts, clues, or information that supports a certain viewpoint or provides proof that a specific situation took place and how it happened. When studying history, historians look to **source materials** as evidence.

Source materials are any **artifacts**, or objects, that were created during or about the time in history being studied. They can include articles, recordings, books, photographs, paintings, and more. We can find source materials on the Internet and in libraries and museums. There are two main types of source materials: **primary sources** and **secondary sources**.

Historians use source materials like pieces of a puzzle. They weave together the information they find in different sources. It can take years for them to gather enough evidence to understand a certain time or event that happened in history.

Because the Second Red Scare was fairly recent, there is a lot of source material available about it. Events that occurred during that era are well preserved in interviews, newspapers, reports, posters, photographs, and more. Modern technologies, such as television and audio recording devices, documented the many different viewpoints of the time. Each of these sources provides a snapshot of North America in the 1950s and 1960s. Together, they help us look back and give us clues as to what people were thinking, feeling, and doing.

▶ During World War II, the Canadian government imprisoned known and suspected communists. On September 23, 1942, the Secretary of the Communist Party of Canada (far left) and other communist leaders met at the office of lawyer J. L. Cohen (far right) to fight for their rights.

ANALYZE THIS

In a time of war, what reasons might the government have had for imprisoning communists? Were these reasons valid? Are some people treated similarly today?

Primary sources are firsthand accounts by people who personally witnessed or took part in events at the time they occurred. You have probably created primary sources of your own. Perhaps you keep a journal or post updates on a social media page. You may have snapped photos of a sports event using your smartphone. These are all examples of primary sources. They tell us about a certain time in history. They can be preserved, stored, and passed down to future generations. E-mails, notes to your friends, and videos of your family vacation are primary sources a historian could one day use as evidence of what life was like in the 21st century.

Written primary sources include:

- Diaries: Books in which people document their personal thoughts
- Journals: Books in which people log details about specific events, activities, or trips
- Advertisements: Descriptions of goods or services that are available to others
- Transcripts: Transcribed text versions of speeches, meetings, and recordings
- Letters: Documents sent between people
- Telegrams: Coded messages sent over long distances using wire signals that are decoded and written down
- Lyrics: Words to songs that people sing
- Blogs: Online journals
- Social media: Websites where people post messages, images, and videos

There are countless primary sources of information about the rise of communism in North America, about the First and Second Red Scares, about McCarthyism, and about its influence on society at the time and in the years that followed. There are telegrams and letters between the people involved, interviews, and transcripts of meetings. The government kept detailed records of all its investigations. In the interests of national security and to not offend Russia, many of these records were sealed from the public at the time they were created, but they have since been released.

PERSPECTIVES

Read the telegram opposite and the response above it. What point of view does McCarthy represent? What point of view does Truman represent? How do they compare?

"When I saw five strapping provincial police enter my home, I experienced an instinctive moment of fear, but I quickly realized that there was nothing I could do but remain silent. They rummaged through drawers and bookcases, removing literature and books. We had to change apartments a few times, because of the raids."

Danielle Dionne, a communist woman and her family who were a target for the Red Squads in Quebec. [Red Squads were police units in the 1950s, investigating communists and political activists.]

Draft

My dear Senator:

I read your telegram of February eleventh from Reno, Nevada with a great deal of interest and this is the first time in my experience, and I was ten years in the Senate, that I ever heard of a Senator trying to discredit his own Government before the world. You know that isn't done by honest public officials. Your telegram is not only not true and an insolent approach to a situation that should have been worked out between man and man but it shows conclusively that you are not even fit to have a hand in the operation of the Government of the United States.

I am very sure that the people of Wisconsin are extremely sorry that they are represented by a person who has as little sense of responsibility as you have.

Sincerely yours,

[HST]

◄ President Truman drafted this response to McCarthy's telegram (below). In it, Truman expressed his distaste for McCarthy and his accusations.

TATE DEPARTMENTS GIVING TO THE CONGRESS ANY INFORMATION IN REGARD TO THE DISLOYALTY OR THE COMMUNISTIC CONNECTIONS OF ANYONE IN THAT DEPARTMENT, DISPITE THIS STATE DEPARTMENT BLACKOUT, WE HAVE BEEN ABLE TO COMPILE A LIST OF 57 COMMUNISTS IN THE STATE DEPARTMENT. THIS LIST IS AVAILABLE TO YOU, BUT YOU CAN GET A MUCH LONGER LIST BY ORDERING THE SECRETARY ACHESON TO GIVE YOU A LIST OF THESE WHOM YOUR OWN BOARD LISTED AS BEING DISLOYAL, AND WHO ARE STILL WORKING IN THE STATE DEPARTMENT. I BELIEVE THE FOLLOWING IS THE MINIMUM WHICH CAN BE EXPECTED OF YOU IN THIS CASE

◄ On February 11, 1950, Senator Joseph McCarthy sent this telegram to President Harry S. Truman. In it, he explains that he knew of 57 communists within the U.S. government.

Have you ever heard the saying, "A picture is worth a thousand words"? Pictures are a type of primary source material known as visual evidence.

Visual primary sources can include:

- Maps: Diagrams that show the features of a certain area of land
- Photographs: Images created using a camera that are printed on paper or stored **digitally**
- Political cartoons: Illustrations or comic strips with a political message
- Posters: Large printed pictures
- Billboards: Large outdoor boards displaying advertisements
- Movies, films, and videos: Moving images recorded by a camera and projected on screens

Events that took place during McCarthy's investigations and the Red Scare are well documented with visual evidence. Cartoonists, such as Herbert Block, used humor to tell a story about the political situation. Senator McCarthy used a large map to show the locations of communist organizations across the United States (see pages 16–17). Posters were often used as **propaganda** to instill a fear of communist activities among the general public. Newspaper photographers and television crews captured important moments such as

▼ The cover of *The New York Times* of March 12, 1954, featured a story about the U.S. Army accusing McCarthy of misconduct.

government hearings and interrogations conducted by McCarthy. Journalist Edward R. Murrow was memorable for his anti-McCarthy news broadcasts on the CBS television show *See It Now*.

In addition to visual evidence, **auditory** evidence—information we can hear that is recorded in various ways—can help historians. You can hear fear, sadness, anger, or joy in a person's recorded voice. You can hear crowds chanting in **protest**, police sirens blaring during a raid, or even silence at a pivotal moment during a testimony. Each of these recorded sounds helps paint a picture of the impact an event has on people's lives. During the Red Scare, the government made recordings of interviews, speeches, hearings, radio and TV addresses, conferences, and even secret meetings.

EVIDENCE RECORD CARD

Anti-communist propaganda during the First Red Scare

LEVEL Secondary source
MATERIAL Comic book
LOCATION United States
DATE 1947
SOURCE Universal History Archive/UIG via Getty Images

▶ This comic book published in 1947 was used to inform people about the threat of communists.

PERSPECTIVES

Who was the intended audience for this book? What is the burning flag meant to illustrate? What emotions does this cover bring out? Why does the comic book creator want people to fear communism?

IS THIS TOMORROW

AMERICA UNDER COMMUNISM!

Secondary sources are created using information found in primary sources. They are a person's description or interpretation of a historical event. That person did not experience the event or situation directly. He or she bases their views on information and evidence provided by those who witnessed the event firsthand.

People who create secondary sources study, **evaluate**, analyze, and interpret primary sources. They often use more than one primary source to form their opinions. Different people will come to different conclusions. They give us new **perspectives** on a situation or event.

Examples of secondary sources include:

- Novels: Fictional books with characters and events that often mirror reality to a certain degree
- Textbooks: Books that contain detailed, factual information about a certain topic
- Magazine or newspaper articles: Pieces of writing about events that took place in the past
- Movies: Stories recorded using movie images that reflect the details of a historical event
- Maps: Modern-day diagrams that show historical information
- Websites: Internet pages that feature information about situations and events
- Biographies: Fact-based accounts of a person's life that is written by someone other than the person featured in the biography
- Interviews: Discussions with subject-matter experts who studied primary sources
- Documentaries: Movies or television and radio programs based on factual events

▼ Released in 2005, *Good Night, and Good Luck* is a historical drama starring George Clooney. It centers on the relationship between radio and television journalist Edward R. Murrow and Senator McCarthy.

david strathairn
patricia clarkson
george clooney
jeff daniels
robert downey jr.
frank langella

we will not walk in fear of one another

good night, and good luck.

"They called Roosevelt a Red, remember, and they said Truman was out to set up Communism in America. ... And that magazine—Blueprint—is a bit on that side, too—they've attacked the mildest kind of liberals as subversive and they're perfectly willing to ruin people without the semblance of a trial or any kind of reasonable investigation."

excerpt from the book *The Troubled Air* by U.S. author Irwin Shaw, 1951

Primary sources are typically created at the time of an event or situation. A secondary source, by contrast, is created any time afterward. Secondary sources about the Red Scare and McCarthyism include biographies, novels, movies, reports, journals, and documentaries. Some were created days after the situation was unfolding. Others are still being created today. These include movies such as *Trumbo* (2015), about Dalton Trumbo, a screenwriter of the Hollywood movie industry **blacklisted** by McCarthy as communist.

▲ *Scandalize My Name* is a 1998 documentary about the impact the Red Scare and McCarthyism had on the African-American community in Hollywood.

ANALYZE THIS

Is *Scandalize My Name* a primary or secondary source? Consider: Did the creator personally experience McCarthyism? Is the creator summarizing other people's information? Was the source created during the events?

▼ Movie producer, artist, and animator Walt Disney is surrounded by family as he lies in a hammock on New Year's Day 1955. In 1947, Disney had been called to testify at a trial against communist sympathizers (see quote on page 23).

INTERPRETATION

"All things are subject to interpretation; whichever interpretation prevails at a given time is a function of power and not truth."

Friedrich Nietzsche, German philosopher, 1844–1900

Historians must analyze source materials to determine if they are valid, useful, and **accurate**. They may look at the credentials of the person or organization that created the source, when it was created or published, and who published it. They also look at the point of view it represents and whether it shapes the information provided. A **biased** source tries to change someone's perspective on a topic.

Bias is when there is a clear show of support for or against something. If a source is biased, the creator has expressed an opinion for or against a certain person, group, or thing. People who create primary and secondary sources may show bias by including some of their personal feelings or beliefs in the source. If a source is **credible**, it will be fact-based and impartial. There are things historians look for that indicate a source is biased:

- Omitted facts
- Positive or negative word choices
- Additional, unnecessary details
- Extreme language
- Emotional connections
- Political views of the creator

Historians have shown that both primary and secondary sources of evidence exhibit bias from people who supported McCarthyism and those who did not. Recognizing and dealing with this bias is part of the story of the Red Scare.

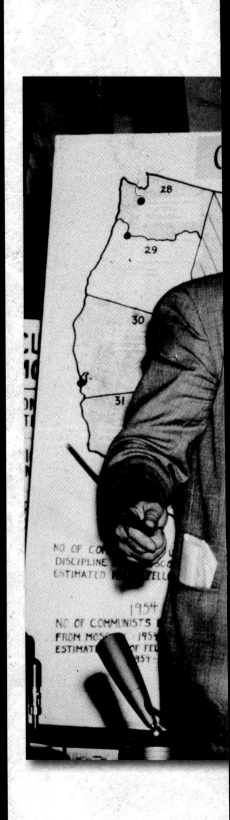

RTY ORGANIZATION U.S.A-FEB. 9, 1950

▲ Senator Joseph McCarthy uses a large map to point out communist organizations across the country as part of his statement against the U.S. Army during the Army–McCarthy hearings in Washington, D.C., in June 1954.

PERSPECTIVES

What does the expression on McCarthy's face tell you about how he was feeling at the time of the investigation? What type of evidence did the map provide? What impact do you think it had on the people McCarthy was speaking to?

ANALYZING BIAS

Historians are like detectives. They must search for evidence to find clues and information from the past. Some of the evidence is relevant, some not. Other evidence can throw them off track or include biased thoughts or ideas.

Historians must take special care when analyzing source materials. They consider the following factors when deciding if a document, image, or artifact offers accurate information about a particular time in history:

- What type of evidence is it—image, transcript—and what does it tell you?
- Who created it—what do you know about this person's credibility?
- When was it created—how long after the event?
- What was happening in the world at the time when it was created?
- What point of view does it represent—the author's, the victim's, simple facts?
- How does the point of view shape the source?

By asking these questions of each source, historians can determine whether it should be included as part of their investigation into the past. Many historians use the Time and Place Rule when analyzing a source. They believe the best sources are created closer in time and place to an event or situation. Sources that contradict commonly accepted facts or information without backup may be less credible.

Context is the circumstances or setting in which a source was created. Context influences people's outlooks or perspectives. Beliefs and customs that were considered acceptable at the time a source was created may not be acceptable 5 or 50 years later or by today's standards.

SPECIAL SENATE INVESTIGATION ON CHARGES AND COUNTERCHARGES INVOLVING: SECRETARY OF THE ARMY ROBERT T. STEVENS, JOHN G. ADAMS, H. STRUVE HENSEL AND SENATOR JOE McCARTHY, ROY M. COHN, AND FRANCIS P. CARR

HEARING

BEFORE THE

SPECIAL SUBCOMMITTEE ON
INVESTIGATIONS OF THE COMMITTEE ON
GOVERNMENT OPERATIONS
UNITED STATES SENATE

EIGHTY-THIRD CONGRESS

SECOND SESSION

PURSUANT TO

S. Res. 189

PART 59

JUNE 9, 1954

Printed for the use of the Committee on Government Operations

WISCONSIN HISTORICAL LIBRARY

 OCT 29 1954

GOVERNMENT PUBLICATIONS

UNITED STATES
GOVERNMENT PRINTING OFFICE
WASHINGTON : 1954

46020°

◄ On June 9, 1954, the U.S. **Senate** released this report outlining the details of charges against McCarthy and others involved in his investigations of communist sympathizers.

McCarthyism and the Second Red Scare took place during the Cold War (about 1946–1991). Following World War II, United States and Soviet governments had very different views about how their countries should be run. The United States was a **capitalist** society with a **democratically** elected government. Americans could own property and create their own wealth. This was in clear contrast to the communist society in the Soviet Union. Some Americans supported the Soviets and their communist ideals. This created a sense of fear that communists were trying to take over North America. Propaganda created during that time in history supported that existing idea and played on people's fears.

◄ There was a **federal** election at the peak of McCarthy's anti-communist campaign. The Republican government knew McCarthy's tactics were extreme, but chose to overlook them because McCarthy was popular with voters. In this political cartoon of 1951 by D. R. Fitzpatrick, the Republican Party (the elephant) is shown with McCarthy (seated) and Republican presidential candidate Robert Taft (standing).

ANALYZE THIS

What do you think were the common beliefs of society at the time this cartoon was created? Were they realistic? What was happening in the world at the time?

"I say that he is as patriotic an American as there can be, and you gentlemen belong with the Alien and Sedition Acts, and you are the nonpatriots, and you are the un-Americans, and you ought to be ashamed of yourselves."

Excerpt from testimony of actor Paul Robeson at the House of Un-American Activities Committee (HUAC) hearings on June 12, 1956

ROOTS OF McCARTHYISM

"There are no morals in politics; there is only expedience. A scoundrel may be of use to us just because he is a scoundrel."

Vladimir Lenin, founder of the Russian Communist Party

Following World War I (1914–1918), the communist movement in North America intensified. Some people felt the capitalist system allowed for wealthy property and business owners to **exploit** workers. In contrast, anyone who was not seen as **patriotic**, such as communists and **immigrants** from Eastern Europe, was considered suspicious.

To make matters worse, soldiers returning home from the war had difficulty getting work while the nation's factories moved from producing weapons to domestic goods. Also, workers demanded more money to cope with **inflation**. Many workers joined labor **unions**, and strikes broke out across the country. Anyone involved was labeled a "Red."

By 1919, the Communist Labor Party of America had been set up. Fears of a revolution like the one in Russia spreading to North America led to the First Red Scare. President Woodrow Wilson's attorney general, A. Mitchell Palmer, ordered authorities to raid the homes and businesses of anyone he saw as a threat to society. For example, about 250 Russian immigrants were deported. With J. Edgar Hoover, Palmer created the General Intelligence Division of the Federal Bureau of Investigation (FBI) to investigate suspected **anarchists**. Thousands of people were detained without cause or legal representation. Most were later released.

Finally, the public got word of Palmer's blatant disregard for **civil liberties**. Many prominent Americans spoke out against the Red Scare. The situation began to settle down by about 1925.

▼ In 1951, Senator McCarthy (seated left) testified before the Senate Foreign Relations Subcommittee that State Department official Philip C. Jessup was a communist sympathizer. President Truman had nominated Jessup to be a member of the U.S. delegation to the United Nations.

PERSPECTIVES

Describe what you see. What do you notice first? What is the setting? What people and objects do you see? What types of evidence were being created?

THE SECOND RED SCARE BEGINS

Throughout the 1920s and 1930s, fears of communist organizations in North America subsided, but they did not disappear entirely. Many people believed the Soviets were engaging in **espionage** across North America.

Following the Winnipeg General Strike of 1919, the Canadian government enacted Section 98 of the Criminal Code, a law used to **suppress** the activities of the Communist Party of Canada (CPC) throughout the 1930s. In 1936, the government revoked the law, sparking new concerns about how to minimize communist activities.

Quebec **premier** and attorney general Maurice Duplessis was extremely **conservative** and opposed to unions. In 1937, he created an act to protect the province against communistic propaganda, also known as the Padlock Act. The act gave local authorities the power to shut down any meeting places used by groups that supported communist ideals, or businesses that produced communist propaganda. Duplessis was known for using the act to charge and jail any person or group he disliked.

PERSPECTIVES

What type of source material is this? Which of these people do you think is the accuser, the defendant, and the defendant's lawyer? Who are the audience?

▼ Former communist Paul Crouch (standing) testified before HUAC against Clarence Hiskey, who was an active member of the Communist Party.

In the United States, a number of communist groups had formed during the **Great Depression** (1929–1939). The U.S. government created the House of Un-American Activities Committee (HUAC) in 1938 to investigate these groups. The committee was to uncover any activities that were considered subversive or un-American in nature, with the potential of imprisoning anyone it exposed.

HUAC's first chairman was anti-communist advocate and politician Martin Dies. Dies supported the **Ku Klux Klan** and even received public praise from the group for his work with HUAC.

WARNING
from the
FBI

The war against spies and saboteurs demands the aid of every American.

When you see evidence of sabotage, notify the Federal Bureau of Investigation at once.

When you suspect the presence of enemy agents, tell it to the FBI.

Beware of those who spread enemy propaganda! __Don't repeat vicious rumors or vicious whispers.__

Tell it to the FBI!

J. Edgar Hoover, *Director*
Federal Bureau of Investigation

The nearest Federal Bureau of Investigation office is listed on page one of your telephone directory.

▲ An FBI poster signed by J. Edgar Hoover warns Americans against saboteurs and spies in the early 1940s.

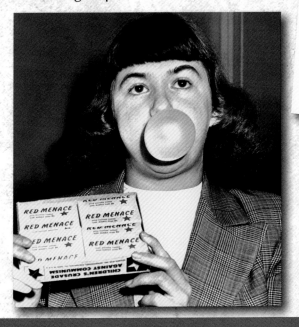

◄ Anti-communist propaganda in the 1950s included chewing gum labeled Red Menace.

"....100 percent Americans, are trapped by this group, and they are represented to the world as supporting all of those ideologies, and it is not so, and I feel that they really ought to be smoked out and shown up for what they are, so that all of the good, free causes in this country, all the liberalisms that really are American, can go out without the taint of communism. That is my sincere feeling on it."

Excerpt from Walt Disney's HUAC testimony about his personal opinion of the Communist Party, October 24, 1947

DISCRIMINATION AND BLACKLISTS

During World War II, the United States, Canada, and the Soviet Union **allied** against a common enemy, the **Axis** forces. But they often disagreed over political issues. The Soviet Union was interested in furthering its communist agenda in Eastern Europe, which democratic North America greatly opposed.

After the war, the United States provided aid to countries that wanted to stop the spread of communism across their borders. Many Americans came to believe the Soviets were operating a spy ring within the United States, raising security concerns across the country. Such fears were not completely unfounded. During World War II, the Soviets were known to use American citizens for espionage. Finally, on March 12, 1947, President Harry S. Truman signed the Truman Doctrine. It ensured economic and military support for Greece and Turkey, which were at immediate risk of communist takeover.

ANALYZE THIS

Blacklisting involved FBI investigators questioning anyone associated with an accused offender—friends, family members, employers past and present, teachers, and more. Why do you think the FBI went to such extreme efforts to expose potential communists? What civil liberties did they violate in the process?

▶ President Truman signed the Truman Doctrine into effect in 1947 to provide aid to any nation experiencing communist pressure.

Nine days later, Truman signed Executive Order 9835 in response to **allegations** that his government was infiltrated by communist spies. U.S. government employees were investigated to ensure they were loyal to the United States. Similar investigations took place at local and state levels of government, and within private companies. Hundreds of people were fired and thousands were forced to resign. In addition, the government issued a blacklist of subversive organizations and people.

As well as government and companies, others began to **discriminate** against people and organizations on the blacklist. Individuals were denied jobs, passports, and bank loans based on the list. Basic rights and freedoms were violated, including the right to be considered innocent until proven guilty, freedom of association, and freedom of speech.

▲ This anti-war leaflet and petition was distributed by American communists in Cleveland in 1950. It suggested the Truman Doctrine in Korea was a threat to world peace.

▶ Anticommunist investigations led to the arrest in June 1951 of the 19 important communists pictured here.

"We will forthwith discharge or suspend without compensation those in our employ, and we will not re-employ any of the 10 until such time as he is acquitted or has purged himself of contempt and declares under oath that he is not a Communist."

Eric Johnston, excerpt from the Waldorf Statement, December 3, 1947

HUAC IN HOLLYWOOD

At about the same time, HUAC launched investigations in Hollywood, forcing 40 actors, directors, producers, writers, and others to expose any communists among them and testify against one another. Movie studios began blacklisting suspected subversives from working in the industry. Hundreds of people lost their jobs and many were not able to return to the industry for more than 10 years. Among them were the Hollywood Ten, including John Howard Lawson. He was the president of the Screen Actors Guild and a Communist Party leader. The 10 were sentenced to a year in prison.

Soon HUAC began touring cities across the country, investigating anyone suspected of being un-American, including teachers, union leaders, and musicians.

By the late 1940s, the threat of communism was far-reaching. In 1949, the Soviet Union launched its first nuclear weapons tests. That same year, Chinese Communist Party chairman Mao

◀ This 1950 cartoon was used as peace propaganda following communist North Korea's invasion of South Korea.

ANALYZE THIS

In 1950, only about 50,000 Americans belonged to the Communist Party. Still, fear of a takeover by the Reds was at an all-time high. What events led to the Red Scare? Why do you think North Americans were fearful of communism? Why did they want to keep it from coming to their countries?

"As one of our outstanding historical figures once said, 'When a great democracy is destroyed, it will not be from enemies from without, but rather because of enemies from within.'"

Excerpt from McCarthy's Wheeling Speech, February 9, 1950

Zedong led his party to power in China. A year later, the Korean War broke out between communist-backed North Korea and South Korea, which received support from the United States and its allies. It seemed to many Americans that communism must be stopped at all costs.

With the Second Red Scare firmly at hand, politicians looked for ways to ease public fears. Hoover and the FBI continued to mount evidence against subversives, which led to the conviction of 12 leaders of the American Communist Party in 1949. They were charged with conspiring to overthrow the U.S. government.

▼ On June 20, 1953, the *Los Angeles Times* ran a story on the execution of convicted Soviet spies Ethel and Julius Rosenberg. They had given away information about the U.S. nuclear weapons project. Senator McCarthy's chief counsel, Roy Cohn, was a prosecutor in the case. He possibly created false evidence against the Rosenbergs.

EXTRA

RACE RESULTS — **Los Angeles Times** — **PICTORIAL**

EQUAL RIGHTS · *LIBERTY UNDER THE LAW* · *TRUE INDUSTRIAL FREEDOM*

| VOL. LXXII | IN THREE PARTS ★★★ | SATURDAY MORNING, JUNE 20, 1953 | 42 PAGES | DAILY, 10¢ |

ROSENBERGS DIE
Pair Executed for Atom Spying

Supreme Court and Eisenhower Reject Couple's Last Pleas

OSSINING, N.Y., June 19 — Atom Spies Julius and Ethel Rosenberg died in Sing Sing Prison's electric chair shortly before sundown today. The executions followed quickly after the Supreme Court set aside a stay of execution granted Wednesday by Justice William O. Douglas and President Eisenhower's refusal to grant them clemency.

SING SING PRISON, N.Y., June 19 (UP) Atom Spies Julius and Ethel Rosenberg were ordered electrocuted late today for betraying their country's secrets to Russia and threatening the lives of millions by bringing the world closer to an atomic war.

The Justice Department set the time for the doomed couple's death in Sing Sing Prison's electric chair after a day of suspense in which the U.S. Supreme Court denied their final appeals and President Eisenhower again refused executive clemency.

Warden Wilfred Denno announced first the husband and wife espionage team would be put to death in the gray-walled prison's death chamber "before sundown," which comes at 8:30 p.m. (5:30 PDT) today at Sing Sing.

Later he said the first execution would come at 8 p.m. EDT, with the second a few minutes later.

END OF TRAIL—Summons to death in electric chair came swiftly for Atom Spies Ethel and Julius Rosenberg after stay was revoked and clemency was refused.

MCCARTHY SPEAKS OUT

Until 1950, Senator Joseph McCarthy had been an unremarkable politician. The former Wisconsin circuit judge and World War II veteran was elected to the Senate in 1946. A Republican, he was fairly inactive for the first three years of his term. That all changed after a speech he gave in Wheeling, West Virginia, when he claimed numerous State Department employees were communists.

Almost overnight, McCarthy became a household name. Though claims similar to his were not uncommon at the time, McCarthy's accusations implied presidents Franklin Roosevelt and Harry S. Truman had supported communist activities within their governments. To add fuel to all this, McCarthy also said he had a list of 205 names to accompany his claims.

McCarthy was called to testify before the Senate Committee on Foreign Relations. The anti-communist senator defended his claims, but he offered only one name as evidence: Professor Owen Lattimore. An expert in Chinese history, Lattimore had worked as a consultant on Chinese affairs during World War II. McCarthy claimed he was a Soviet spy. Despite the fact that no evidence

PERSPECTIVES

What jobs do you think the people in this picture have? What documents do you think they were reading? What are they doing there? Who is the audience for their work?

"We must remember always that accusation is not proof and that conviction depends upon evidence and due process of law. We will not walk in fear, one of another. We will not be driven by fear into an age of unreason, if we dig deep in our history and our doctrine, and remember that we are not descended from fearful men — not from men who feared to write, to speak, to associate and to defend causes that were, for the moment, unpopular.'"

Reporter Edward R. Murrow's response of March 9, 1954, to McCarthy's accusations was ever found in support of McCarthy's claims, Lattimore continued to be investigated over the next four years.

In the meantime, McCarthy kept on pointing fingers at people he believed were subversives. Each time he gave a speech, the number of people on his accused list changed, first to 81, then to 57. McCarthy played on people's fears to build upon and reinforce the atmosphere of fear during the Second Red Scare.

▲ Owen Lattimore (left) held a press conference at his lawyer's office in Washington, D.C., on April 21, 1950, to address McCarthy's allegations.

"Communism is no longer a creeping threat to America. It is a racing doom that comes closer to our shore each day. To resist it we must be intelligently strong."

Excerpt from Joseph McCarthy's speech explaining the communist threat on June 2, 1950

▲ This D. R. Fitzpatrick cartoon of 1948 illustrates the Soviet attempt to drive Western powers—the United States, Britain, and France—out of Berlin, Germany.

MCCARTHYISM REACHES ITS PEAK

Though many people in government disagreed with McCarthy's over-the-top accusations, the general public believed he was a true patriot. They hoped that he would bring an end to the communist threat in North America.

McCarthy was re-elected in 1952 and soon after was named chairman of the Committee on Government Operations of the Senate Permanent Subcommittee on Investigations (PSI). He spent the next two years investigating any government officials who seemed to have even the most remote communist connections.

▼ This 1950s billboard sponsored by the Food Industry for America encouraged people to beware of the communist threat in the nation.

Picture Parade

SEPT. 1953

◄ This 1953 comic book cover instilled fear of Russia dropping a nuclear bomb on America.

McCarthy was relentless in his pursuit, but he never actually found evidence of any communists among the people he interviewed. Still, many people who were investigated lost their jobs and faced harsh criticism from their peers. Those who opposed McCarthy saw him as a witch hunter who paid little regard to the civil liberties of the people he accused of being communist sympathizers.

With a solid team that included Senator Robert F. Kennedy and chief counsel Roy Cohn, McCarthy began investigating anyone he felt had a communist tie. Many Americans believed that if McCarthy said a person was communist, then it must be true. He conducted more than 100 investigations and closed-door interrogations but voters still supported him. It seemed he was unstoppable. His actions became known as McCarthyism, a term first used by cartoonist Herbert Block in a political cartoon on March 29, 1950. Block was not a McCarthy supporter.

"I think the greatest asset that the Kremlin has is Senator McCarthy."

Excerpt from President Harry S. Truman's reaction to the Loyalty Investigation, March 30, 1950

SOCIETY FIGHTS BACK

"On one thing the Senator has been consistent. Often operating as a one-man committee, he has traveled far, interviewed many, terrorized some, accused civilian and military leaders of the past administration of a great conspiracy to turn over the country to Communism."

Excerpt from Edward R. Murrow's *A Report on Senator Joseph R. McCarthy* on *See It Now*, March 9, 1954

McCarthyism led to widespread fears across the United States. On one hand, people feared for themselves. McCarthy's reach was wide, and it seemed no one was safe. On the other hand, fears of communists in North America were also widespread and provoked by the **media**.

Throughout his investigations, McCarthy used extreme tactics, and his accusations became more and more intense to maintain his position in the limelight. Finally, in March 1954, CBS TV's *See It Now* aired two episodes on McCarthy, exposing his abuse of power. Though the show's host, Edward R. Murrow, was opposed to communism, he believed McCarthy's investigations were unfounded. Murrow criticized McCarthy's violation of innocent people and their civil liberties in an effort to bring McCarthy's reign of terror to an end.

In April, McCarthy appeared on the TV show and claimed Murrow was communist. Most Americans had a great respect for Murrow. They trusted him to present an unbiased and impartial report. Murrow later commented on McCarthy's appearance on his show, pointing out errors in McCarthy's statements and claims. Murrow reassured viewers that he himself was not a communist but merely someone who believed in preserving the rights and freedoms of all Americans. The tides had turned for Senator Joseph McCarthy.

▶ These documents show how the wording of resolutions introduced by Republican senators to discipline McCarthy were refined and modified. McCarthy was charged with failure to cooperate with a Senate subcommittee.

[Insert No. 2 on page 1 of 8, Res. 30

ITALIC

Sec. 2. The Senator from Wisconsin, M_
ducting a senatorial inquiry intemperately a
executive hearings in which he denounced, a
the executive branch of the Government, Gene
an officer of the United States Army, for re
his superior officers and for respecting off_
executive directives, thereby tending to dest
which must be maintained between the executiv
branches in our system of government; and the
denunciation of General Zwicker by Senator Mc
of a Senate subcommittee and censures him for

PERSPECTIVES

Read the text of the attachments to the resolution. What do the vocabulary and tone of the texts tell you about the feelings of the senators. What do they accuse McCarthy of doing? Do you think these are key sources for a historian of the Second Red Scare?

EVIDENCE RECORD CARD

U.S. government resolution
LEVEL Primary source
MATERIAL Typewritten document with handwritten notes
PUBLICATION U.S. Senate
DATE November 9, 1954
SOURCE National Archives and Records Administration

83D CONGRESS
2D SESSION
legislative day, JULY 2), 1954

CALENDAR NO. 2540

S. RES. 301

[Report No. 2508]

IN THE SENATE OF THE UNITED STATES

JULY 30 (legislative day, JULY 2), 1954

Mr. FLANDERS submitted the following resolution; which was ordered to be printed **NOV 9 1954**

ported by Mr. Watkins, from the select committee created pursuant to order of the Senate of August 2, 1954, with amendments

mit the part struck through and insert the part printed in italic]

RESOLUTION

Resolved, That the conduct of the Senator from Wisconsin, Mr. McCarthy, is unbecoming a Member of the United States Senate, is contrary to senatorial traditions, and tends to bring the Senate into disrepute, and such conduct is hereby condemned.

[Insert on page 1 of S. Res. 301]

No. 1

ITALIC   **ITALIC**

the Senator from Wisconsin, Mr. McCarthy, failed to cooperate with the Subcommittee on Privileges and Elections of the Senate Committee on Rules and Administration in clearing up matters referred to that committee which concerned his conduct as a Senator and affected the honor of the Senate and, instead, repeatedly abused the committee and its members who were trying to carry out assigned duties, thereby obstructing the constitutional processes of the Senate, and that this conduct of the Senator from Wisconsin, Mr. McCarthy, in failing to cooperate with a Senate committee in clearing up matters affecting the honor of the Senate is contrary to senatorial traditions and

in con-
eleased
esenting
Zwicker,
iticize
and
faith
ative
vows the
airman

ARMY–MCCARTHY HEARINGS

In the weeks following Murrow's exposé on McCarthy, the senator's popularity began to decline. April 22, 1954, marked the first of 36 days of televised hearings during which McCarthy was set to investigate allegations that the U.S. Army was "soft" on communism.

McCarthy's accusation came on the heels of a request the army refused to provide special treatment to one of McCarthy's former investigators who had been drafted into the army. McCarthy was brought up on charges, and as a result, he stepped down as the chairman of the Committee on Government Operations of the Senate PSI during the hearings. Coupled with Murrow's report, McCarthy's reputation weakened. Still, he played a key role in the U.S. Army investigations.

During the hearings, the public got to see McCarthy in action for the first time. He often interrupted the investigations if answers were not favorable to him. Many thought his claims were unfounded.

▼ People across the country tuned in to watch the televised Army–McCarthy hearings in 1954.

"I felt that if the public could see just how McCarthy operated, they would understand just how ridiculous a figure he really was."

Excerpt from ABC network President Leonard Goldenson's 1991 memoir on his decision to air the Army–McCarthy hearings

Others, such as many members of the Catholic Church, believed McCarthy was trying to protect the country from a legitimate communist threat. In many ways, the country was divided on the topic and his methods.

The hearings were the first of their type to be televised, and people were drawn into the drama unfolding on their screens. ABC broadcast more than 188 hours of footage at a cost then of $600,000. The network could barely afford it, but gambled anyway. It paid off, and ABC got about 20 million viewers.

At first, McCarthy began investigating claims of espionage at Fort Monmouth, New Jersey. As the weeks dragged on, however, his focus shifted to an army dentist who had refused to answer questions asked by the committee. This new line of questioning was not well received by the army. Thirty days into the hearings, McCarthy's reputation was clearly waning.

▼ McCarthy reads an ad paid for by the United Electrical Workers Union.

"I bring out the worst in my enemies, and that's how I get them to defeat themselves."

Roy Cohn, Chief Counsel of the Permanent Subcommittee on Investigations (PSI)

ANALYZE THIS

The U.S. United Electrical Workers Union was targeted by McCarthy for communist ties during the Red Scare. Why do you think McCarthy is smiling while he reads this ad?

CASE CLOSED

After years of his anti-communist investigations, McCarthy had met his match. Army lawyer Joseph Nye Welch had squelched every one of McCarthy's accusations throughout the hearings. On June 9, 1954, McCarthy accused Welch of employing a young lawyer with communist affiliations. Welch responded with the infamous line, "Have you no sense of decency, sir, at long last? Have you left no sense of decency?"

McCarthy attempted to rebuke Welch's question, but Welch stopped McCarthy short by asking for the next witness to be called. For a moment there was silence in the room. Then the crowd of citizens and reporters erupted in applause. McCarthy's only response was to turn to Roy Cohn and ask, "What happened?" Within days, the hearings ended, and not one of McCarthy's claims had been substantiated.

Later that year, the Republicans lost control of the Senate, and McCarthy was removed as the chairman of the Committee on Government Operations of the Senate PSI. On December 2, 1954, the Senate voted 67 to 22 to **censure** McCarthy for misconduct. Though the majority of his peers voted in favor of censuring him, McCarthy received some

PERSPECTIVES

This photo was taken on November 11, 1954. How many different signs can you see? What do they say and who and what are they supporting? What do you notice about the protesters' expressions? How do you think they are feeling?

"*Until this moment, Senator, I think I never really gauged your cruelty or your recklessness.*""

Joseph Nye Welch in an excerpt from U.S. Army–McCarthy hearings, June 9, 1954

▲ A crowd of McCarthy supporters gathered at Pennsylvania Station in New York City before boarding a train to Washington, D.C., to protest the senator's proposed censure.

support from others, who chose not to vote for his censure. The only Democratic senator who did not provide public support for McCarthy's censure was future U.S. president John F. Kennedy, brother of Robert F. Kennedy (see page 31).

McCarthy received little attention from the media or his political peers after his censure. Some members of the media, such as radio broadcaster Fulton Lewis, Jr., continued to support McCarthy, even when their audience declined. McCarthy died in 1957 of liver failure after turning to alcohol. Yet he is still well known for his intense use of fear mongering among the general public and attacks on innocent people. Even today, the term *McCarthyism* is often used in association with any person or group that openly accuses people of wrongdoings without proper evidence. Though McCarthy may be gone, his legacy lives on.

(see page 31).

ANALYZE THIS

McCarthy was given a state funeral that was attended by 70 senators. Thousands of people visited his body before he was buried. What does this tell you about the nation's feelings at the time?

▼ On December 3, 1954, *The New York Times* featured a front-page story about McCarthy's censure—along with other Red Scare news.

President Rejects Blockade Of China Now as Act of War

But He Pledges No Let-Up in Efforts to Free 13 Americans Jailed by Peiping— Holds Truce Obligates U. N. to Act

By JOSEPH A. LOFTUS
Special to The New York Times

East Bloc Says Joint Army Will Counter Bonn in NATO

By CLIFTON DANIEL
Special to The New York Times

ATOM POWER SEEN AS COMMON IN 1976

Half of All Electric Plants Then Building Will Use It, G. E. Head Tells N.A.M.

By A. H. RASKIN

EISENHOWER WARNS G. O. P. RIGHT WING; CHIDES KNOWLAND

Insists Party Must Follow a Progressive Course or Face Loss of Influence

Transcript and summary of the news conference, Page 18.

By WILLIAM S. WHITE
Special to The New York Times

FINAL VOTE CONDEMNS M'CARTHY, FOR ABUSING SENATE AND COMMI ZWICKER COUNT ELIMINATED IN DE

RANCOR CONTINUES

Welker Refuses to Let Flanders Apology Go Into the Record

By JAMES RESTON
Special to The New York Times

CONDEMNED ON TWO COUNTS: Senator McCarthy as he left the Senate floor last night after members adopted a resolution condemning his conduct. The vote was 67-22.

PRESIDENT ALERTS MAYORS ON ATTACK

Cities Are Front-Line Targets,

SENATORS CLEARED ON M'CARTHY MAIL

Inquiry Indicates Request

REPUBL

Democrat in Suppo Again

HISTORY REPEATED

"When you say I don't care about the right to privacy because I have nothing to hide, that is no different than saying I don't care about freedom of speech because I have nothing to say."

Edward Snowden, former Central Intelligence Agency (CIA) employee who leaked classified information to the public, May 22, 2015

In the late 1950s, laws relating to the Red Scare were overturned by the U.S. Supreme Court, and the blacklist was lifted. However, on January 5, 1957, President Dwight D. Eisenhower announced the United States would provide military or economic aid for any Middle Eastern country resisting communism.

In April 1961, the United States unsuccessfully invaded Cuba to counter that country's links with Russia. Cuba gave the Soviets permission to place missiles there in 1962. After a U.S. spy plane spotted the missiles, the United States formed a blockade of ships in an effort to prevent the Soviets from shipping more missiles to Cuba. Finally, after 14 days, the two countries agreed to a peaceful resolution. The Cuban Missile Crisis was over.

The late 1960s and early 1970s saw the United States heavily involved in the Vietnam War, which tried— unsuccessfully—to stop communism spreading in Southeast Asia. Fears of communist ideology were still firmly cemented in U.S. society in the 1980s. President Ronald Reagan offered military support to forces fighting against communism in Nicaragua, Afghanistan, and Angola.

In May 2013, a computer scientist and former CIA worker, Edward Snowden, became a household name when he leaked classified documents from the National Security Agency (NSA). His revelations showed the U.S. government had been spying on Americans and on other governments. The situation has been compared to McCarthy's investigations.

Why do you think Snowden did not appear live at the South by Southwest Interactive session? In this photo, what is in the background behind Snowden?

▼ Edward Snowden used Google Hangout to make an appearance at a South by Southwest Interactive session in the United States on March 10, 2014.

Through a series of newspaper interviews in Hong Kong, Snowden revealed that the NSA, in partnership with major U.S. telecommunications companies, had been collecting data on ordinary Americans. He was charged with violating the Espionage Act and theft of government property. Snowden sought **asylum** in several countries and finally settled in Russia.

CLOSING BORDERS AND NATIONAL SECURITY

The Edward Snowden story is just one example of how McCarthyism has influenced modern-day society in America. Another is the war on terror. On September 11, 2001, terrorist group Al-Qaeda attacked the United States. The attack killed 2,996 people and made the nation fearful of terrorist threats. A month later, the U.S. government passed the Patriot Act. Aimed at strengthening domestic security, the Act gives authorities the power to monitor phone calls and e-mails, collect financial records, and track Internet activity of anyone it thinks suspicious.

Soon after President Donald Trump took the oath of office in 2017, he signed an executive order into effect that temporarily barred people from seven predominantly Muslim nations from entering the United States. The idea behind the travel ban was to give the government time to develop a better **refugee vetting** system to stop terrorists from entering the country. Much like the Red Scare, the act was made to protect the United States from an external threat. But it also limited the freedoms of people within the country. The Supreme Court later overturned the ban.

Other acts in North America have tried to limit the actions of people believed to be a threat to society. The Alien Registration Act of 1940, or Smith Act, made it illegal for anyone to seek to overthrow the government. Ten years later, the Internal Security Act, or McCarran Act, required all communist organizations to register with the government. Immigrants belonging to those groups were not allowed to become citizens.

Studying the source materials of these acts, old and new, connects us with McCarthyism and the Red Scare.

▲ Chaos broke out at border crossings and airports across America following the president's travel ban on January 27, 2017. Many people gathered at airports to protest the executive order.

"I think that Mr. Snowden raised some legitimate concerns. How he did it was something that did not follow the procedures and practices of our intelligence community. If everybody took the approach that I make my own decisions about these issues, then it would be very hard to have an organized government or any kind of national security system."

Quote from German media outlet *Der Spiegel* interview with Barack Obama

PERSPECTIVES

Who do you think are protesting here, and what are they trying to achieve? What parallels do you see with banners, posters, and newspaper headlines related to McCarthyism and the Red Scare?

ANALYZE THIS

The United States fought the Korean and Vietnam wars on the basis of the "domino theory"—the idea that if one country became communist, surrounding countries would soon do the same. Do you think the current U.S. government believes in the domino theory?

◀ After years of shunning Cuba for its communist affiliations, Cuban President Raul Castro and U.S. President Barack Obama met at the United Nations Headquarters in New York City on September 29, 2015.

"We cannot let the wrong people in and I will not allow that to happen during this administration."

President Donald Trump

TIMELINE

March 1917 Russian revolution begins

1917

November 1918 World War I ends

1919 to 1920 The Palmer Raids take place, triggering the First Red Scare

October 29, 1929 Great Depression begins

1938 House of Un-American Activities Committee is created

1945

May 1945 World War II ends in Europe

August 6, 1945 United States drops the first atomic bomb on Hiroshima, Japan, ending World War II in Asia

1946 Joseph McCarthy is elected to the Senate

March 12, 1947 Truman Doctrine is announced

March 21, 1947 Executive Order 9835 comes into effect

August 1949 Soviet Union explodes its first atomic bomb

1950

October 1, 1949 China becomes a communist nation

February 9, 1950 During a speech in Wheeling, West Virginia, McCarthy alleges 205 government workers are communist sympathizers

March 29, 1950 Political cartoonist Herb Block coins the term *McCarthyism*

June 25, 1950 to July 27, 1953 Korean War takes place

1952 McCarthy is re-elected and named chairman of the Committee on Government Operations of the Senate Permanent Subcommittee on Investigations

March 1954 Edward R. Murrow denounces McCarthy on The CBS show *See It Now*

December 2, 1954 McCarthy is censured

1955

April 22, 1954 Army–McCarthy Hearings begin

1956

January 5, 1957 Eisenhower Doctrine is established

February 1959 Fidel Castro seizes power in Cuba

April 30, 1975 South Vietnam falls to the communists

December 1979 Soviet army invades Afghanistan

October 26, 2001 Patriot Act is created

January 2017 President Donald Trump announces a travel ban on people from seven predominantly Muslim nations

2017

November 5, 1955 to April 30, 1975 Vietnam War takes place

October 14 to 28, 1962 Cuban Missile Crisis occurs

February 1976 Soviets and Cubans install communist government in Angola

December 1991 Collapse of the Soviet Union signals the end of the Cold War

May 2013 Edward Snowden reveals the NSA is spying on Americans and on other governments

World map showing communist influence during the Second Red Scare era

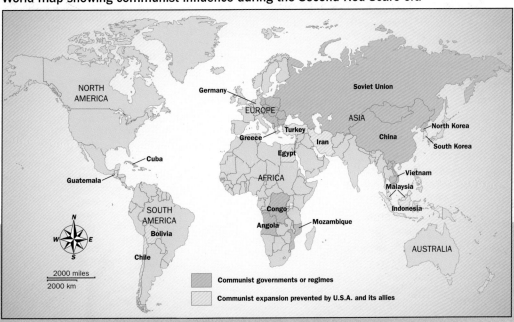

NORTH AMERICA
Germany
EUROPE
Soviet Union
ASIA
Turkey
Greece
China
North Korea
South Korea
Iran
Egypt
Cuba
Vietnam
Guatemala
AFRICA
Malaysia
SOUTH AMERICA
Congo
Indonesia
Angola
Mozambique
Bolivia
Chile
AUSTRALIA

N W E S

2000 miles
2000 km

Communist governments or regimes

Communist expansion prevented by U.S.A. and its allies

BIBLIOGRAPHY

QUOTATIONS

p. 4 Edward R. Murrow quote: Walker, Charles George. My Few Wise Words of Wisdom. Millennium, December 2000, p. 137.

p. 6 J. Howard. McGrath quote: Fariello, Griffin. Red Scare: Memories of the American Inquisition. W.W. Norton & Company, December, 2008.

p. 8 John Adams quote: The Portable John Adams. Penguin Books, 2004.

p. 10 Danielle Dionne quote: "The Red Scare," CBC Learning: http://www.cbc.ca/history/EPISCONTENTSE1EP15CH1PA2LE.html

p. 14 Shaw, Irwin. The Troubled Air. Random House, 1951.

p. 16 Friedrich Nietzsche quote: Chang, Larry (ed.). Wisdom for the Soul: Five Millennia of Prescriptions for Spiritual Healing. Gnosophia Publishers, 2006.

p. 19 Paul Robeson quote: "Paul Robeson Appears Before HUAC," June 12, 1956. http://historymatters.gmu.edu/d/6440/

p. 20 Vladimir Lenin quote: BrainyQuote.com, Xplore Inc, 2017. https://www.brainyquote.com/quotes/quotes/v/vladimirle135580.html.

p. 23 Walt Disney quote: "Testimony of Walter E. Disney," October 24, 1947. http://historymatters.gmu.edu/d/6458/

p. 25 Eric Johnston quote: Bresler, Robert J. Freedom of Association: Rights and Liberties under the Law. ABC-CLIO, 2004, p. 170.

p. 26 Joseph McCarthy quote: Speech of Joseph McCarthy, Wheeling, West Virginia, February 9, 1950. http://historymatters.gmu.edu/d/6456

p. 28 Edward R. Murrow quote: "A Report on Senator Joseph R. McCarthy" on See It Now, March 9, 1954. http://www.lib.berkeley.edu/MRC/murrowmccarthy.html

p. 29 Joseph McCarthy quote: "Speech Explaining the Communist Threat." TeachingAmericanHistory.org, June 2, 1950. http://teachingamericanhistory.org/library/document/speech-explaining-the-communist-threat/

p. 31 Harry S. Truman quote: "Reaction of President Harry Truman to Loyalty Investigation, News Conference at Key West," March 30, 1950. http://historymatters.gmu.edu/d/8078/

p. 32 Edward R. Murrow quote: Finkelstein, Norman H. With Heroic Truth: The Life of Edward R. Murrow. iUniverse, 2005, p. 9.

p. 34 Leonard Goldenson quote: "50 years ago, TV helped to end McCarthyism." Today.com, June 8, 2004. http://www.today.com/popculture/50-years-ago-tv-helped-endmccarthyism-wbna5165583

p. 35 Roy Cohn quote: Safire, William. "Essay; About Roy Cohn." The New York Times, August 4, 1986. http://www.nytimes.com/1986/08/04/opinion/essay-about-roy-cohn.html

p. 36 Joseph Nye Welch quote: "Have You No Sense of Decency." The Army–McCarthy Hearings. June 9, 1954. http://historymatters.gmu.edu/d/6444/

p. 38 Edward Snowden quote: "Edward Snowden: NSA reform in the U.S. is only the beginning." The Guardian, May 22, 2015. https://www.theguardian.com/us-news/2015/may/22/edward-snowden-nsa-reform

p. 40 Barack Obama quote: Spiegel Interview with U.S. President Barack Obama. Spiegel Online, November 18, 2016. http://www.spiegel.de/international/world/spiegel-interview-with-us-president-barackobama-a-1122008.html

p. 41 Donald Trump quote: "Trump: We want a 'big, beautiful open door,' but not for 'the wrong people'." Washington Examiner, February 13, 2017. http://www.washingtonexaminer.com/trump-we-want-a-big-beautifulopen-door-but-not-for-the-wrong-people/article/2614698

TO FIND OUT MORE

Brooks, Philip. The McCarthy Hearings. London: Heinemann, 2003.

Giblin, James Cross. The Rise and Fall of Senator Joe McCarthy. Boston: Clarion Books, 2009.

Levine, Ellen. Catch a Tiger by the Toe. New York: Viking, 2005.

Malaspina, Ann. The McCarthy Era: Communists in America. New York: Chelsea House, 2011.

Rall, Ted. Snowden. New York: Seven Stories Press, 2015.

Sheinkin, Steve. Most Dangerous: Daniel Ellsberg and the Secret History of the Vietnam War. New York: Roaring Brook Press, 2015.

INTERNET GUIDELINES

Finding good source material on the Internet can sometimes be a challenge. When analyzing how reliable the information is, consider these points:

- Who is the author of the page? Is it an expert in the field or a person who experienced the event?
- Is the site well known and up to date? A page that has not been updated for several years probably has out-of-date information.
- Can you verify the facts with another site? Always double-check information.

- Have you checked all possible sites? Don't just look on the first page a search engine provides. Remember to try government sites and research papers.
- Have you recorded website addresses and names? Keep this data so you can backtrack and verify the information you want to use.

WEBSITES

Spartacus Educational
Get a detailed look at Senator Joseph McCarthy and the Red Scare.
http://spartacus-educational.com/USAmccarthy.htm

United States Senate
Read the complete five-volume collection of transcripts and information from the Army–McCarthy Hearings.
https://www.senate.gov/artandhistory/history/common/generic/McCarthy_Transcripts.htm

Diefenbaker Canada Centre
Learn all about Canada's role during the Cuban Missile Crisis.
https://www.usask.ca/diefenbaker/virtual-exhibits/cuban-missile-crisis.php

History Matters: The U.S. Survey Course on the Web
Search for complete transcripts from HUAC and McCarthy investigations on subversives and communists.
http://historymatters.gmu.edu/

Encyclopedia Britannica
Read about the life and career of Senator Joseph McCarthy.
https://www.britannica.com/biography/Joseph-McCarthy

Duckster's The Cold War Red Scare
Learn more about the Red Scare and McCarthyism.
http://www.ducksters.com/history/cold_war/red_scare.php

The Cold War Museum
Find out more information about Joseph McCarthy and McCarthyism.
http://www.coldwar.org/articles/50s/senatorjosephmccarthy.asp

Library of Congress
View a collection of Herb Block's political cartoons about the Red Scare and McCarthyism.
https://www.loc.gov/exhibits/herblocks-history/fire.html

GLOSSARY

accurate Correct in all details

allegations Claims, often without proof, that someone has done something wrong or illegal

allied Supported one another

analyze Examine closely

anarchists People who want self-government without a state to interfere

archives Places that store historical information about a location, a person, or an event

artifacts Objects made by human beings

asylum The offer of protection by a nation to someone fleeing harm

auditory Related to the sense of hearing

Axis The name for the group of nations (Germany, Japan, and Italy) that fought against the Allied powers

biased Prejudiced in favor of or against one thing, person, or group

blacklisted Added to a list of people or businesses thought to be suspicious

Bolshevik Member of the Communist Party in Russia

capitalist An economic and political system in which trade and industry are privately owned

censure A formal expression of disapproval

citizens People who have full rights to live in a country

civil liberties Freedoms granted to individuals for the good of society, such as the right to free speech and religion

class A division of people based on their wealth or social status

Cold War A long period of mistrust, rivalry, and non-violent conflict between the United States and the Soviet Union, and their allies that lasted from 1946 to 1991

communist An economic and political system in which all property is owned by its members and is used for the good of all people

conservative Acting or approaching a situation with more caution than most would use

context The circumstances in which an event happens

credible Something that can be believed

democratically Using a political system in which government is made up of representatives elected by all adult citizens

digitally Related to computers and associated technologies

discriminate Treat with less favor than someone else

economy The wealth and resources of a country

espionage The use of spies, usually by governments, to gain political and military information

evaluate Judge the value of something

evidence Information or objects related to an event

expedience When something is helpful or useful in a situation to achieve a quick result

exploit Make full use of

federal Something that is part of the U.S. government and is not under the control of a state or city

Great Depression A period of economic recession that started in 1929 and lasted until late in the 1930s

ideology A system of ideas and ideals on how a country should be run

immigrants People leaving onea country to live in another country

infiltrate Secretly find a way into a group

inflation Rise in the cost of living

Ku Klux Klan A white supremacy group that uses terror to support its cause

leftist A person who wants to reform the existing government and who supports social equality

media The press, TV, radio, and Internet

patriotic Showing love or devotion for one's country

perspectives Points of view or ways of looking at something

premier In Canada, the head of government of a province or territory

primary sources Firsthand accounts or direct evidence of an event

propaganda Information, often misleading or biased, used to promote a particular point of view

protests Showing strong feelings against something

refugee A person who has been forced to flee his or her own country because of war or disaster

revolution An uprising of the people to force a major change in government

secondary sources Materials created by studying primary sources

Senate One of two parts of the U.S. government that makes the laws; part of Congress, along with the House of Representatives

socialist Following a collective or government ownership and running of society

society A group of people forming a single community with its own distinctive culture and institutions

source materials Original documents or other pieces of evidence

spies People employed by a government or other organization to secretly obtain information about an enemy or competitor

subversion The act of overthrowing, destroying, or undermining an existing or established system

suppress To stop, weaken, or keep in check

sympathizers People who agree with someone else's beliefs or politics

unions Groups of workers who join together to resolve labor issues with the owners of businesses

vetting Evaluating for possible acceptance

World War I War fought from 1914 to 1918 between the U.S., Canada, the U.K., France, Italy, Japan, and their allies against Germany, Austria-Hungary, the Ottoman Empire (Turkey), and their allies; The U.S. entered in 1917

World War II War fought from 1939 to 1945 between the U.S., Canada, Britain, the U.S.S.R, and their allies, against Nazi Germany, Italy, Japan, and their allies; The U.S., U.S.S.R, and Japan did not join until 1941

INDEX